Book D

Does your child misbehave every chance they get? Are they always arguing and questioning your orders and requests? Do they deliberately throw tantrums to get the things they want? Is your first instinct always to yell, scream, or tell them no?

If so, then you need to change the way you parent!

Many parents think that they have it all figured out when it comes to parenting. They think that using punishments and other verbal abuses gets things done. They know how to fight back during arguments and conflicts, and assume they get their way. However, this isn't the best model of parenting. Your child shouldn't obey you out of fear. They should because they know it is the right thing to do. Positive disciplining can help teach them this difference.

In this book, we review what positive discipline is and how we can put its techniques into practice. We see how it can help parents improve communication and make interactions with their kids more fulfilling and meaningful. We look at seven vital parenting skills needed to facilitate parents to start with positive parenting.

These include the following:

- Identifying the reasons behind misbehavior and how to prevent it.

- How being empathetic can help both parents and children.
- Why offering choices can go a long way when preventing misbehavior.
- Creating a YES environment to enhance confidence and self-esteem.
- Redirections and how they work towards improving child behavior.
- How treating mistakes as lessons can serve as a great opportunity to teach about resilience.
- How being consistent and clear about expectations can prevent misbehavior from the get-go.

Aimed to be a simple yet interesting read, this brief guide offers you everything you need to get started with the principles of positive discipline.

7 Vital Parenting Skills for Improving Child Behavior and Positive Discipline

Proven Positive Parenting Tips for Family Communication without Yelling or Negativity

Frank Dixon

Before we begin, I have something special waiting for you. An action-packed 1 page printout with a few quick & easy tips taken from this book that you can start using today to become a better parent right now!

It's my gift to you, free of cost. Think of it as my way of saying thank you to you for purchasing this book.

Claim your download of Profoundly Positive Parenting with Frank Dixon by scanning the QR code below and join my mailing list.

Sign up below to grab your free copy, print it out and hang it on the fridge!

Sign Up By Scanning The QR Code With Your Phone's Camera To Be Redirected To A Page To Enter Your Email And Receive INSTANT Access To Your Download

Before we jump in, I'd like to express my gratitude. I know this mustn't be the first book you came across and yet you still decided to give it a read. There are numerous courses and guides you could have picked instead that promise to make you an ideal and well-rounded parent while raising your children to be the best they can be.

But for some reason, mine stood out from the rest and this makes me the happiest person on the planet right now. If you stick with it, I promise this will be a worthwhile read.

In the pages that follow, you're going to learn the best parenting skills so that your child can grow to become the best version of themselves and in doing so experience a meaningful understanding of what it means to be an effective parent.

Notable Quotes About Parenting

"Children Must Be Taught How To Think,
Not What To Think."

— Margaret Mead

"It's easier to build strong children than to fix
broken men [or women]."

- Frederick Douglass

"Truly great friends are hard to find, difficult
to leave, and impossible to forget."

— George Randolf

"Nothing in life is to be feared, it is only to be
understood. Now is the time to understand
more, so that we may fear less."

— Scientist Marie Curie

Table of Contents

Introduction

Parenting—a skill that comes highly underrated. Think about it, isn't it odd that you get paid to go to work, drain your energy, get those juices flowing in your brain to concoct a great business plan, strategy, or perhaps birth a new idea that will change the lives of many; you get credited for it in the form of a promotion, an upgrade on your car or house, or receive bonuses big enough to plan another trip with the spouse and the kids, and yet, when it comes to parenting—the most important job in the world—we fall short on our praises.

We see a kid throwing a tantrum in the grocery store and we instantly blame the mom or dad for bad parenting. But do you know the backstory? Do you know how embarrassed they are to not be able to control their children's behavior? Do you know how terribly they want to discipline their children, but know that it would only worsen the tantrum?

Heck, you must have had a day like this too? A day where nothing seems to go according to the plan. The kid has been cranky since the morning, acting up, whining over little things. They are being pushy and testing your limits. To make them feel a little better, you think about taking a trip to the grocery store together, hoping it will lighten their mood and make them happy. And then it happens... They have their eyes set on something unhealthy or way too expensive or unnecessary and the next minute they are rubbing their toes, pulling out their hair, and crying at the top of their lungs.

And this is just a normal day in the life of parents. Imagine how difficult it must be to deal with them when they get sick and resist taking the medications? Or days when they won't get ready for school and want to skip it by faking a stomach ache.

So our question is this: why is there no prize, bonus or recognition? Isn't this the most important job?

Since modern-day parenting is becoming more and more challenging, and children are becoming harder to handle, there has emerged a new concept that suggests modeling good behavior using positive praise instead of all the yelling and shouting we normally do.

Positive Discipline.

Positive disciplining techniques are proven more effective than traditional parenting techniques in many ways. They promise improved behavior, a strengthened bond, and a calm and composed parent that isn't stressed about what the next day will bring.

Therefore, in this next book in the series, we plan to prep the parents with seven vital parenting skills needed to implement positive disciplining techniques and raise kids that are not only disciplined but also happier, confident, and empathetic.

Without wasting any more time, let's dive right into it.

Chapter 1: What is Positive Discipline?

"How to discipline my child" is one of the most widely searched terms on Google. It shows how desperate we all are to look for ways to discipline them. But if you ever notice, none of the websites, at least the most reliable ones, ever suggest punishments and negative reinforcements to instill discipline. Traditionally, we all thought it was a sure-fire way to teach manners, but new research suggests the opposite. Punishments do more than just physical or emotional damage. They affect the brain. Kids that are brought up in families where punishments and abuse have been considered a norm for disciplining children have raised mentally unstable, aggressive, and antisocial adults (Durrant & Ensom, 2012; Ohene et al., 2006; Smith, 2006).

So how do we discipline them if punishments are out? Well, you aren't the only parent grappling with that thought. Children of today are sensitive. They struggle with competition as well as social anxiety both online and offline. Despite knowing that, we are all guilty of screaming and yelling on our children.

That leaves us with only one thing—a new approach!

Enter positive discipline.

Understanding Positive Disciplining

The concept of positive discipline is based on a model first introduced by Alfred Adler and Rudolf Dreikurs. Dr. Adler, in 1920, introduced this unique idea of parenting in the United States. He believed that when children are treated respectfully, they behaved well. He also pointed out that leniency doesn't mean allowing them to do whatever they wanted to, and thus drew a clear line between spoiling them and respecting their wishes. Dreikurs and Adler wanted parents to adopt a kind and compassionate approach to teaching.

Later, based on the same principles, Jane Nelson, who was the director of the project Adlerian Counseling Concepts for Encouraging Parents and Teachers (ACCEPT), a federally-funded project that received excellent feedback in its developmental phase, self-published a book in 1981. It was called "Positive Discipline." Later, in 1987, it was published by Ballantine.

Research from recent studies confirms that children are hardwired from birth to connect with others. They have been doing it before birth—in the womb too. They want to have a sense of belonging, want to be pampered, and looked after and play a key role in shaping the community. Children that are able to connect with their parents, peers, and educators from an early age exhibit fewer behavioral problems.

Positive Discipline focuses on developing a strong and deep relationship between the parent and the child that is based on mutual respect and communication. It focuses on teaching parents to teach their children not just the *what* of things, but also the *why*. Positive disciplining uses approaches such as kindness, empathy, compassion, and respect. There are five important criteria for positive discipline:

- The first is being kind yet firm at the same time. This means that you have to guide your child towards the right behavior but also be firm and definitive.
- The second is promoting a sense of significance and belonging. This involves helping them with opportunities that allow them to connect with you and the family.
- The third is looking for effective solutions in the long run. The goal shouldn't only be to prevent misbehavior in the present, but to eliminate the bad habit altogether. This requires that we offer children solutions that are positive and acceptable to exhibit instead.
- The fourth is teaching valuable life and social skills. We must encourage our children to respect others, show concern for them, be accountable, problem-solve, corporate, and contribute at home and in the community.
- And finally, introduce kids to their own skills and talents so that they know how to use them in constructive ways.

The Perks of Disciplining Children Using Positive Parenting

When we allow kids to become active participants in their behavioral development, it teaches them independence and builds their self-esteem. This improves communication in the house as everyone feels like they're part of a team, equals. There is also the establishment of trust between the parent and child that further strengthens their bond in the future, especially when they enter adolescence.

Multiple studies prove the benefits of positive parenting and disciplining. According to one, positive discipline reduces the instances of childhood depression (Dallaire et al., 2006). The study focused on how different traditional parenting styles led to an increase in mental health issues in children when they became adults, and how positive discipline proved promising. It also talked about how being a disciplinarian led to increased stress levels in parents, and how they unintentionally pass it on to their children.

Some additional benefits of positive parenting and why parents of today should stick to it are discussed below.

Promotes Happiness and Boosts Self-Esteem

When the focus is on positive action and the child feels valued and cared for, it can lead to greater levels of happiness. When they feel included and important, their self-esteem also improves. When the focus is on encouragement of good behavior as opposed to discouraging the bad, the child develops a positive outlook towards life. They start to view mistakes as opportunities, and lacking and imperfections as normal and acceptable. They are more willing to try new things as there is no fear of punishments (Weintraub, 1998).

And as for the parents, this approach can reduce stress and promote happiness. There are fewer clashes over who gets to have the final say in things as both the parent and the child are aware of the expectations that have been set. Also, when there are fewer conflicts, parents can finally experience some peace of mind and prevent themselves from becoming overwhelmed by negative thoughts.

Eliminates Power Struggles and Negative Behavior

Sometimes, children try to get away with negative behavior using techniques like crying or whining. However, when you try to discipline them positively, you have to remember to set limits for them. At the same time, you have to focus on positive behavior instead of the negative, and offer positive alternatives. When children know of these ways, they are less likely to disobey you, and gradually, their bad behavior diminishes. It also leads to fewer arguments and fights between you and your child, suggests Natasha Becker, the self-published bestseller author and mother (Becker, 2019).

Makes for Effective Communication

Effective communication is one of the most essential components of positive disciplining. It is the very goal of this parenting approach. It allows us to communicate with our child in a positive and action-oriented way instead of yelling or punishing them for negative behaviors. Being positive encourages children to come forward and share their feelings because they know that they will be listened to and not judged or insulted. They know they won't be talked down and screamed at for having opinions. When children feel encouraged in this way, it develops a trusting relationship between the parent and the child (Building Trust through Communication with Teens, 2013).

Chapter 2: The Seven Vital Parenting Skills for Improving Child Behavior

All kids are unique in their way. Some are shy and introverted, while others can bring the whole house down with their energy and spirit. Some are empathetic and kind while others value power more than the love of others. Some want to be accepted by others while some don't like it when praised. Some want to explore the whole world while others enjoy living in their little bubble. Some are big with temper tantrums and stress out their parents while others are calm and subtle with their demands. Some are dreamers who see things imaginatively while others like to follow their peers and forebearers. Some are procrastinators and have things done last minute while others like to stick to their notes and play by the rules. Some want to be independent and crave more freedom while others like to be pampered all the time. Some want to have their way in everything and want more control over decisions related to them, while others want to have things decided for them.

Children, with their different personalities and types, make the world a better place to live. Their smiles, their laughter, happiness, and success are what we live for. We want to see them happy and accomplished. We want them to have the things we never had and want to be protective of them. We want them to have meaningful relationships growing up, friends they can always count on, and role models in the form of their teachers, coaches, and mentors. We want them to dream big and follow their passions with confidence. We want them to have successful careers, good finances, and peace of mind.

It all begins with good social skills and your parenting style. Social skills include skills like communication, listening, empathy, problem-solving, accountability, and positivity. It is our role to teach them how to hold proper conversations, behave well and be presentable, regulate their emotions in healthy ways, be accepting of others, be responsible and own up to their mistakes.

However, we can only teach these lessons if we adopt the right parenting style to begin with. If our children feel that we are too strict or too overprotective, they start to feel suffocated. They begin craving more privacy and independence and stop being transparent with us. On the other hand, if we are too carefree, they think that we couldn't care less about them and feel neglected.

Our parenting approach has to be positive and compassionate. We have to deal with them and their problems with a progressive and open mind. We have to lay the right foundations to let them soar high and aim for the skies using good social skills.

Positive discipline or positive parenting has shown promising results in the upbringing of today's children. They want more freedom, and this approach to parenting supports that. They want to do things their way but still have some rules to follow; positive discipline offers this. They want to feel valued and validated, and positive parenting offers that too. They want someone to pat them on their backs for a job well done, and voila, it offers that too. If we go back to chapter one and review the five important factors we discussed, this modern-day approach to parenting seems like the perfect package to improve communication, strengthen family bonds, and improve child behavior.

All that said, adopting positive parenting as the ultimate approach requires a set of skills. This is where our seven vital parenting skills come in. They are aimed at facilitating this approach to parenting simply and strategically. Before we get started with them in detail, let's unveil what they are and what they represent briefly in this chapter.

Vital Parenting Skill #1: Find Out the Reasons for Misbehavior

Misbehavior doesn't happen out of habit. There is usually an unmet need or desire which compels children to act negatively. The first parenting goal or skill is to identify that trigger or cause and then use it to prevent misbehavior from happening.

Vital Parenting Skill #2: Don't be Mean—Be Empathetic Instead

All parents must be empathetic towards their kids as it allows them to form closer bonds and improve family relations. Since the goal is just that, it can be a great skill to nurture.

Vital Parenting Skill #3: Offer Them Choices

Let kids have choices because when they do, they feel included and valued. Under this parenting skill, we shall look at how having choices empowers children, and minimizes negative behaviors.

Vital Parenting Skill #4: Stop Saying No

Most parents don't know about the negative influence the word "no" has on their kids. When their needs are repeatedly declined with a flat no, they lose confidence and develop poor self-worth. Thus, as parents, we have to create a YES environment for them to feel confident and motivated to take on new challenges, build resilience, and become self-reliant.

Vital Parenting Skill #5: Redirect, Redirect, Redirect

Redirection or distraction involves strategically moving the child from a negative or unsafe situation to a safer and more positive one. This parenting skill enables parents to prevent misbehavior from escalating, as well as lower the chances of a conflict or argument.

Vital Parenting Skill #6: Treat Every Mistake as a Learning Opportunity

Mistakes are nothing but disguised opportunities. We need to teach our kids to start viewing them as lessons and stay motivated instead of giving up or feeling shame and guilt. We need to prepare them for the worst and encourage mistake-prone attempts because it means they are at least trying.

Vital Parenting Skill# 7: Be Consistent with Expectations

The final parenting skill that all parents must possess or nurture in themselves is clarity. Children need structure and clarity in their lives. If we expect certain behavior from our children, we need to let them know of it from the start. We have to lay down the right foundations so that they don't get confused, forget instructions, or end up making mistakes.

Chapter 3: Parenting Skill #1 Find Out the Reasons for Misbehavior

Whenever children act out or misbehave, they are trying to tell us how they are feeling. It is often a sign that something isn't right with them and they are trying to seek our attention. They have been doing so since birth. Remember the time when they were little and short of words? How did they communicate? They cried, stomped their feet on the ground, clapped their hands, and screamed.

Thus, when the goal of parenting is to improve behavior, the most logical thing to do first is to determine the reasons for the misbehavior.

Have you ever taken medication without a proper diagnosis? To treat and prevent misbehavior, the first thing you need to do is figure out why they are acting the way they are, only then moving on to the preventive measures.

Why do They do What They Do?

When figuring out which disciplining strategy would work best for your child, find out what is causing them to act out of their character. Some of the most common reasons include:

Trying to Get Your Attention

Sometimes, we fail to realize how little time we have for our children. We stay busy at work all day and then come home to get busy cleaning, cooking, and then preparing things for the next day; we forget our children need us too. Spending time with our children, playing games with them, supervising their homework, and conversing with them is hardly ever on our to-do list. When children notice this, they start doing things that would get your attention. Naturally, we are quick to respond to negative things. For example, we may fail to praise them on cleaning up a table but we will surely point out their messy eating manners. Thus, children learn that negative behaviors are the way to get your attention and they resort to them.

Testing Your Limits

Children also try to test your limits and patience. When they are told to refrain from something, it piques their curiosity. They want to know if you are serious about the consequences you talked about or if you just bluffed. They want to know what will happen if they break the rules and whether you are consistent with agreed punishments or not. They test you to know if there is a possibility that you bluffed and they can get away with things.

Lacking Social Skills

Sometimes, children also misbehave when they lack social skills. For instance, your child may have a hard time sharing their toys with other kids or waiting for their turn because they don't know how to play collaboratively. Thus, they would try to hit another child and snatch the toy from their hands instead of waiting or their turn.

Being Unable to Control Emotions

When children don't know what to do about the big and unwanted feelings they are going through (such as sadness, failure, anger, disappointment, or even excitement) they act out to seek attention from their parents or others to guide them through. We must introduce healthy ways of coping with negative feelings from the start so that they don't feel overwhelmed.

Having Unmet Needs

Children, when young, don't know how to be direct with their needs and demands. In households where parents are disciplinarians, children often shy away from discussing their needs and hesitate in telling their parents about them directly. For example, if they are still hungry, after eating dinner, they might act out but not come clean about their needs to eat more. If they are tired but don't want to go to bed, they might act out because, although their body wants to rest, they don't. An unmet need can be another reason why they misbehave.

Wanting Freedom

Children also misbehave when they want to feel included in decisions about their lives. They may want to pick out a dress for themselves and have the final say. They may want to be asked what they would like for dinner rather than just given something to eat. They might want the freedom to decide things for themselves, and when they feel their parents are trying to take that away from them, they disobey. They want to do things themselves, even if they aren't yet capable of them. Ever noticed how they want to wear makeup or drink from a full-size cup because they think they are all grown up? When we stop them from doing so, disobedience follows.

Preventing Misbehavior from the Get-Go

Once you have determined what causes all that anger and frustration to come out as chaos, your goal is to identify the triggers and act before they induce bad behavior. For instance, if you know that your child will have a hard time sharing his toys with other kids, be proactive, and don't give the other children toys that your child most loves playing with. Let your child have them to themselves so that a fight can be prevented. Prevention is one of the best techniques for discipline. Arguments and tantrums don't just start right away. They gradually build their tempo. You have to prevent it before it happens. It may seem difficult at first, but it is an investment you will be glad you made.

Here are a few ideas to get you started.

Have clear Rules

When children know how to behave and what is expected of them, they are more likely to act that way. If you are taking them outside and you expect them to not run away on the streets, let them know that it is forbidden before they leave the door. Be very clear and direct so that they fully understand the rules.

Let Them Know of the Consequences

Similar to the first point, you also want them to know about the aftermath of behaving badly. They should know what awaits them if they act out. Once clear rules have been set, they must know of the consequences if they don't abide by the rules. They will be less likely to test your limits or challenge you by deliberately breaking them.

Offer Structure and Routines

A structure or set routine about the day's tasks can also prevent misbehavior. Create a chart of every day chores, include how they will spend their free time so that they follow it. Be consistent with the schedule and don't allow too many changes, as children will see those changes as opportunity. Routines, if provided correctly, can soon turn into habits. For example, if they know they need to brush their teeth before getting into bed every night, they will start to do it out of habit after a week or two.

Teach Delayed Gratification

Delayed gratification or impulse control allows children to wait to have a bigger reward in the end. We all know of the marshmallow test (Mischel et al., 1972). Children who are taught to control their impulses and not give in to their temptations are more likely to show control over their emotions too (Morin, 2019). This will prevent many power struggles and temper tantrums.

Appreciate Good Behavior

We all love to be praised and recognized for our work. We want the applause, the pat on the back and being told that someone is proud of us. Well, kids want that too. Most of their childhood revolves around getting your approval and appreciation. They want to impress you. They want to be appreciated for their effort. Doing so, not only gives them a sense of accomplishment, boosts their confidence and self-esteem but also increases the likelihood of repetition of that behavior. Therefore, whenever you catch them doing something good, be appreciative.

Knowing why they misbehave and how to prevent it before it happens, is a great strategy to deal with misbehavior in children altogether. If we put the strategies to work, we are bound to notice a difference in the way they behave—hopefully, in a positive manner.

Chapter 4: Parenting Skill #2: Don't be Mean—Be Empathetic Instead

Empathy makes us feel more connected and understood. We all want support from our loved ones. We want them to understand what we are going through, to listen to us with a calm mind and open heart, and not to judge us for our choices and decisions. Children are born empathetic, however, if they don't show compassion as they grow older, a lot of the blame can be put on the lack of opportunities provided by the parents, or the absence of a role model. Some may even say that ever-increasing competition and exposure to violence, crime, and peer pressure, has led to our children to become unsympathetic towards others. They see it as a sign of weakness, and so are quick to judge those who open up to others and want to be heard.

But what if we told you that teaching your child to be empathetic is one of the greatest gifts you can give them?

Empathy allows us to be able to hear someone, feel their pain, experience what it is like to be in their shoes, and see them for who they are—not for their actions. Empathy keeps us from judging others, while lending them our support and ear.

The Power of Empathy

But that still doesn't answer the question: why do our kids need empathy?

When we teach our children about empathy, we help them enrich the relationships they share with us and others. That leads to amazing things happening. Teaching empathy allows them to form deeper connections with everyone and offers valuable insights into the experiences of others. Experiencing what the other person is experiencing helps them step out of reactivity and form better responses.

When a child is empathetic, they are also better at regulating their own emotions. It promotes the art of reasoning, and rational thinking too. It also helps them deal with the everyday stresses they face, and view the world with a more positive outlook. Research proves that compassionate people are better at handling stress and unexpected circumstances than their non-empathetic friends. Empathetic people are also happier and less anxious (Henry et al., 1996). It also makes people more social and interactive. For many kids, this means the formation of new and strong friendships. Being compassionate is also a likable trait: children who have it are more attractive than others. Empathy may not make them the *most* popular kid in their class, but they surely will be someone everyone would like to hang out with.

How to be More Compassionate

The goal is not only to teach compassion and empathy but to model it so that it rubs off our children too. When they see us being compassionate towards them and, importantly, others, they start to see us as role models. They get inspired and wish to be more like us. Why? Because everyone likes people who are compassionate and kind. It is something that requires effort and patience and not everyone has it. So it becomes a valuable trait to have.

When the question is how we can be more compassionate and empathetic towards our children to improve family relationships and communication, here are a few tips that help.

Be Kind to Them

How would you want to be treated if you go up to someone to share your feelings? You would expect them to listen to you with an open mind, not pass judgment, not try to fix things for you, nor say things that seem disrespectful or insulting. Our children want the same. Therefore, whenever your child comes up to you after they have done something wrong, don't turn them down by yelling or humiliating them. Would you have liked it if someone did the same to you? Treat others how you would want to be treated.

See Things from Their Perspective

If your children come up to you for something, it means they want to be heard and guided. This isn't the time to scold or ground them. You need to take their feelings into account and try to understand why they did what they did. When children don't know how to deal with big emotions, say jealousy, envy, or pain, they experiment with things to find relief. So if your child tore his favorite shirt into pieces because everyone at school laughed at him for wearing it, don't scold them for it. Try to be supportive and see things from their perspective. Let them know that you understand how they must have felt and that you understand why they did what they did. Sometimes, they only need that.

Ask, Don't Presume

We all give away some non-verbal cues to let the other person know how we are feeling. When we are angry, we have a disgruntled look on our faces, when we are sad, our eyes water, when we are in pain, we make sounds like "ouch," or "oh." These are all non-verbal cues that children also give to let others know that they are struggling. Sometimes we misinterpret these cues. It is always wise to be on the safe side and be sure of what your child is going through and what they need. Let them explain things themselves instead of assuming things on your own and making things worse.

Validate Their Feelings

When we empathize with children, we normalize the emotions they feel. We may have our own opinions, and may not agree with the way they figure things out; letting them go with their plans and not intervening takes courage. That is what we want to teach our children too. As a parent, you have to know that even when they are overreacting or taking a wrong turn, you encourage them to go forward with it. Their feelings are important and if they feel strongly about something, you have to support them.

Don't Judge

A reaction is a natural response to an action. If we are being yelled at or receiving some harsh words, we are bound to react. However, when we choose to respond with empathy and not let our emotions take over, we let our children know that reactions don't always have to come first. We show them that patience and thinking rationally are more important. This is only possible when you stop for a minute, and keep from judging your child for an outburst or tantrum. You allow them to vent their frustration without reacting in the same manner, choosing instead to respond with compassion.

Introduce "I" Statements

Statements that begin with "you" feel defensive and harsh. Statements that begin with "I" seem less harmful and direct. I statements can start a conversation without starting the blame game.

For instance, you may want to burst out at them with statements like, "You are too careless. You never pay attention to anything I say." However, when you substitute something like this, "I feel disrespected when you act carelessly, ignoring the things I tell you to do," you leave some room for a decent conversation to happen, as this approach is less threatening. There is a better chance that the child will be willing to hear more about what you have to say instead of shutting you out emotionally because they feel disrespected or humiliated.

Don't Try to Fix Things

As a parent, we understand that you don't want to see your child get hurt or make decisions that are going to end in pain and suffering. However, one of the most crucial rules of being empathetic is to not try to fix things. Going into let-me-fix-this-for-you mode may seem right, but it doesn't always mean your child will be happy. Sometimes, they just need someone to vent their problems too. They just want to feel lighter and better. Only offer help or advice if they ask for it specifically.

Be an Active Listener

Being empathetic requires active listening. Active listening means that you give the speaker your undivided attention, full concentration, and read their mind. It involves paying attention to not just their spoken words but also their gestures, body movements, tone, and facial expressions. You have to listen not just to what they are saying but also to what they aren't saying. When we listen actively to our children, we make them feel truly heard. It makes the speaker feel respected and shows that they are valued.

Practices that allow us to develop and show empathy are of great value. We must, as parents, teach these to our kids too. Since they are known to be great imitators and look up to us, we are the best chance at helping them develop compassion for others and respect for themselves. So let's do it right and raise them as compassionate, kind, and well-behaved kids.

Chapter 5: Parenting Skill #3: Offer Them Choices

To make good and sound decisions, we need both practice and failure. We need to know what we did wrong the first time to be able to avoid it in the future. More practice also sharpens our minds and gets us thinking of new, more efficient ways to do things. It is a necessary skill to have. Another way to make better decisions is with choices. When we have more than one thing to choose from, it urges us to think sensibly and pick the one with greater benefits. Sometimes, those benefits come in the form of reduced time, less effort, fewer steps, and greater profits. Choices help us differentiate between the good and the bad and also between rewards and consequences. If we want our children to make better decisions and learn to problem-solve themselves, we have to give them several options to choose from.

In this chapter, we look at how offering kids with choices helps build their confidence and self-worth as they not only feel valued but also validated. In the first part, we talk about a particular connection between choices and behavior—if there is any; and in the second part, discuss scenarios where giving choices to our children makes them better at decision-making and improves their behavior.

How Having Choices can Minimize Misbehavior

Being a parent with a busy schedule, having a pre-planned routine offers peace of mind. With a plan in the process, we make decisions for our children and expect to see them follow through. However, this isn't always in their best interest as it limits their ability to think freely and become self-reliant. We want them to grow up confident and handle their affairs themselves. That includes making as many as a hundred decisions per day or more. When decisions are made for them instead of with them, they feel less empowered. Conversely, having choices can go a long way. You can always start with simpler choices like what they would like to do, take a bath or a nap, eat a fruit or a veggie, do their homework before playtime or after it, etc.

The goal is to let them think rationally and choose wisely after pondering over the pros and cons of each choice. There are multiple benefits to giving them choices.

Prevents Temper Tantrums

What are most of the temper tantrums about? They are about gaining more control over their lives and activities. Your kid isn't deliberately trying to be hard, they just want a sense of control. When was the last power struggle you had with your kid? Was it over applying peanut butter before jam on a peanut butter and jam sandwich or was it because you poured their milk for them when they wanted to do it themselves? Most tantrums happen over stupid events, but the reasons they happen aren't stupid. Children need a bigger say in the matter that concerns them. When offered choices, they feel more in control and special. They feel that their decision matters, and that changes the whole game. If you are trying to minimize outbursts, giving options is a good start.

Enhances Problem-Solving Skills

Not all decisions taken by your child will have a fruitful or rewarding outcome. Some of their choices might even make them suffer, such as choosing to eat out instead of having something healthy, which can lead to digestive problems. However, since they made that choice, they have to deal with the consequences too. This type of parenting not only teaches them about responsibility but also encourages them to find solutions once things have gone haywire. This means that it can force them to change their current state and seek means that will bring relief and happiness. This is where problem-solving comes in. The next time they are given the same options to choose from, they are going to choose the one with a positive reward. Meaning, they may choose to eat healthily.

Builds Their Confidence

When allowed to make decisions for themselves, children feel confident. When they decide something and it ends well, they feel proud of themselves and elevated. To encourage the habit, start with simple choices to get their morale high, then let them have a say in bigger matters, for example, as to how they would like to spend their free time, or what they would like to wear or eat.

Cultivates a Sense of Worth

One of the most neglected areas of parenting is making your kids feel valued. In reality, kids are more perceptive and creative than adults. Thus, it is wrong to assume that they won't make good choices for themselves. When we offer them choices, we are telling them that we acknowledge their wisdom and knowledge. This can improve their self-worth, and they will be less likely to misbehave as doing so would mean losing the opportunity to have a choice.

Teaches Accountability

When children make their own decisions, they have no one to blame but themselves when things go wrong. This teaches them about accountability and how to own up to their blunders, and face the consequences of their actions. Additionally, offering them choices teaches them to act responsibly: they need to control their impulses and think logically in order to make choices that don't have bad consequences. This also boosts their cognitive development.

Smart Ways to Give Your Kids Choices

Depending on your parenting style, there are various ways to offer your kids choices. The earlier we encourage them to make sensible decisions based on smart choices, the sooner they will learn to be independent. Before you know it, they will have no trouble relying on their sound judgment.

Here's how you can make them ready for the world out there and promote confidence and rational thinking.

Let Them Choose Which One

This is one of the smartest ways to get them to do things. You simply have to ask them to pick one of two or more choices and let them have the final say. When given the choice between things like reading or doing math, cleaning the windows or helping set the table, putting the dishes in the dishwasher or folding the laundry, etc., whichever choice they pick, they will at least have to do one of the two things.

Give Them the Option to Choose Their Clothes

Kids, when growing up, want to play by their own rules. They are seeking a new identity for themselves.

Dressing a certain way is usually one of the many things that allow them to express themselves as unique individuals (Rasicot, 2019). If they are nerdy and shy, they may not want to dress up like their peers. Let them choose as long as it isn't too provocative, statement-making, or questionable. As long as they look decent and well-dressed, don't try to force your opinions on them. This isn't the battle you need to pick, as it will go on forever. Let them decide how they wish to portray themselves.

Give Them the Choice to Decide When They Want to do Something

Again, being too opinionated or strict with the rules can promote misbehavior. Since the goal is to minimize it, ask them if they would like to do something right now or at a later time. For example, you can ask them if they would like to change into their nightdress now or after five minutes. If you notice carefully, it still implies that the action has to be taken. It just leaves them with the choice to decide when they want to do it. Chances are, they are going to pick later, but that should work for you too, as long as they stick to their promise.

Give Them Choices Between Foods

Their health is a prime concern. You want to feed them with the best, but that isn't always possible. However, with choices, you can let them have their way as well as feed them something nutritious and healthy. Choices between different types of foods, like between different vegetables or breakfast items, can also minimize tantrums. You don't have to cook them exactly what they want, rather, ask them to choose between the two things you are ready to prepare. For instance, if there is rice and soup available for dinner, you can ask them to pick one. Or you can ask them to choose between a buttered or toasted bread, a bowl of salad or beans, etc.

Let Them Choose an Activity

Let them have a say in what they want to do with their free time. Of course, as a parent, you would want them to do something productive or imagination-building, but let them decide what they want to do. You can always suggest things like painting or reading, playing basketball or making a puzzle. You can even direct their choices by being more specific, like asking whether they would like to play a monopoly or another board game. If they are younger, you can ask them to decide if they would like to walk to the park or ride in the stroller. When they feel more in control, they act out less.

Chapter 6: Parenting Skill #4: Stop Saying No

Go back to when you were a kid. Can you recall the times you were told no? How did that make you feel? Did it not feel disheartening and demotivating? Now think about how your child must feel when you do the same? The word "no" is mostly the first-word children pick up when they start speaking. It isn't because it is simple and has only one syllable. It is because it is one of the most repeated words they hear. Some evidence suggests that a one-year-old hears the word "no" at least 400 times per day (Aria, 2008). Hearing no can be stressful for both the parent and the child. When parents say no to their children, they know they are discouraging them from things they are interested in or want to do. When children hear the word no, it affects their confidence and self-esteem. They feel devalued and unimportant. They also feel neglected, and start to believe that their parents aren't interested in them.

Thus to reduce stress, strengthen the bond between a parent and a child, a positive environment is essential. A positive environment is one where the child hears less of the word no and more of the word yes.

Children are born with an inquisitive and curious nature. They want to discover new things, gain more experience, and safely explore their surroundings. When we repeatedly put them down by saying "no," we unintentionally kill their natural curiosity. We take away their confidence and make them feel worthless. As they grow older, they become more independent and want to push limits. However, when parents bind them with the burden of the word "no," they may feel suffocated. They may also begin to see their parents as their enemies and become distant.

The Importance of Creating a YES Environment

Just to be clear, a Yes environment doesn't mean that we never use the word no in front of our children. We still have to for safety and health reasons. However, what's unique about a Yes environment is that we don't limit or neglect exploration. We promote it. We use the term, Yes to address behavioral concerns. We use it to model good behavior and to fortify communication and interaction. We don't want children to hide things from us or keep secrets. We don't let them go behind our backs and do things we wouldn't approve of. We want them to be more open with us and see us as their mentor and friend. This is only possible if we provide them with opportunities that promote happiness and confidence in them, not diminish it. When we say yes to a child, not only do we boost their confidence, but we also empower them to be more comfortable expressing themselves. Ask yourself this: if you keep saying no to your child repeatedly, do you think they will continue to come up to you, continue to inquire? Saying yes also shows our appreciation for the ideas that take birth in their heads. When we allow them to do the things they want to do, we show them that we are interested in their interests and happy in their happiness.

A Yes environment also prevents misbehavior as we willingly allow the child to have what they want. Thus power struggles and temper tantrums are minimized. But it all seems rather theoretical. Is it practical, and can we break the habit of saying no?

Cultivating a YES Environment— The How-to

There are many ways to create a Yes environment. However, the biggest challenge isn't creating a Yes environment, it's turning a toxic and strict environment of No into Yes. The reason many parents find it difficult is because we are so used to the term no. In many cases, it comes out as a natural response. That is the habit we need to kill as we know how damaging the word no can be to their self-respect and confidence. To get you on the right track, here are a few examples and strategies to create a more positive and encouraging environment for your children.

Give Your No A Valid Reason

Children are inquisitive. They want to know the science behind things. They want to know the *whys*.

Therefore, at times, when they misbehave, like pull your hair or hit you, instead of just screaming "no," tell them why you are saying it. Tell them that pulling your hair or hitting you causes pain. Tell them that you feel hurt when they do it and see if they stop doing it or not. This is a more positive and calm way to handle things without going into a full power-struggle mode. It also tells them that you aren't shouting at them, but objecting to the behavior they depicted. It can also build empathy in them as they wouldn't want to intentionally hurt you.

Let Them Be Kids

They are going to be chaotic. They will run to your dresser to apply your makeup, get in kitchen cabinets to take out the pots and pans, open the fridge to find themselves something to eat or drink, etc. How many times are you going to stop them? Besides, you can't always be running after them, saving them from trouble. You have to give them independence and control. You have to empower them to be able to initiate things on their own. When you continuously reject their ideas and choices, and scream at them for things that count as a mere exploration on their part, you undermine their confidence and self-worth. A yes environment doesn't have to be this toxic. To create one, be proactive. If they have the habit of sneaking into the cabinets, place things that aren't costly or are of no interest. For instance, there is less chance that a child would be interested in playing with rags and mops. If they are after your makeup, put stuff that you don't use or wouldn't mind getting broken or misused. That way, you won't have to say no to them and be able to create a more inspiring and positive environment.

Saying Yes can Increase Happiness

The habit of saying "no" is too common and natural that sometimes we say no without even giving a child's request any thought. How many times did you say no to playing hide and seek because you just didn't have the strength to? How many times did you say no to a fun activity because you were worried about the potential mess it would lead to? How many times did you say no when your child wanted to go to the park but you didn't want to? We bet a lot of times!

However, if you want to create a Yes environment, know that you will have to put their demands first. As the goal is to minimize bad behavior using positive disciplining, let them do the things they want to as long as they are within the limits set by you. Why? It is because you are not only going to make them happy but also feel happy yourself. Chances are you will have more fun in the park than you expected if you give in to their request to go there. Not to mention, giving in to their little wishes can strengthen the bond between you two.

Save your Noes

The word "no" must have effectiveness and significance. When you say it too often or over everything, it loses that importance. It should be used sparingly and only for rather serious things. This will teach them to respect a no, and they will become more obedient when it is used. When we save the word for important occasions, it keeps it meaningful like a full and final order. There is no room for argument left after a sparsely used no.

Get Organized and Smart

Creating a Yes environment will become impossible if there are more than 100 different toys to choose from. Go Marie Kondo and limit the choices they have. Keep in mind that the more items there are, the bigger the tantrum and outburst will be when they are told to clean up after playing. Worst still, you may have to clean up afterward in case the child feels sleepy or has moved on to another activity. From the start, let them have a few things to play with instead of saying yes to taking out every last toy from the toy basket.

The more interested we are in the things they do and the more willing we are to cultivate a favorable and encouraging environment for them, the more they will behave. If we look at the strategies mentioned above, they should help you get started and offer them an environment that prevents the need for misbehavior altogether.

Chapter 7: Parenting Skill #5: Redirect, Redirect, Redirect

Redirection or distraction are great disciplining techniques intended to modify a child's bad behavior and prevent it from happening again. Redirection is the opposite of punishment. It involves relocation or engagement in another activity—something more healthy, safe, and positive. Redirection prevents the outburst of negative emotions and saves the parents from having to say "no" repeatedly to their children. We already talked about the dangers of saying the word "no" in the last chapter, which is why we need to focus more on how to distract them to safety without causing a scene. Psychologists like J. Burton Banks believes strongly in the redirection approaches. In one of his books coauthored by two others, he suggests that redirection can help children modify their behaviors from being inappropriate to appropriate (Esther Yoder Strahan et al., 2010).

How do Diversions Work?

Diversions, distractions or redirection works simply. We all know that children have a short attention span when they are young. They are also quick to become angry and frustrated which usually ends with a temper tantrum or an outburst of crying. Using their short attention span, we remove them from the activity they are engaged in and onto another without them fussing. For example, if they have mistakenly taken up a knife in their hands and are running around the house pointing it at everyone, there are two ways to handle it. Either you run after them, take it from them and scold them for being careless, or you distract them with something as equally interesting as the knife and hope that they give up the knife on their own in the pursuit of the other thing. For instance, you can take up a spoon, show it off a little, talk about how it is better and more useful than the knife, and make them want to give up the knife for the spoon.

There are many benefits of redirection. For example, it can ease physical pain. With our brain's limited ability to focus, it is hard for us to take note of all the things happening around us at once. We need to be wise about what we choose to focus on and why. As limiting as this sounds, we can use it to our advantage. We can use it to distract ourselves from pain and discomfort. The same thing applies to kids. If they have just fallen flat on their face and you know they are about to cry any second, use those few seconds to distract them from the pain and sudden shock to something more pleasant and rewarding. Similarly, you can use the same technique when you take them to the doctor for vaccination shots, and turn their negative experience into a positive one by distracting them to focus on something other than the needle piercing their skin.

But most importantly, for younger children, it can prevent misbehavior from escalating. The minute we see our kids getting out of control or becoming aggressive or frustrated, we know what's about to come next. By pulling their attention elsewhere, we can nip the outburst right in the bud before it even begins. It can help parents avoid situations that soon become out of their control and lead to embarrassment, such as when they are in a grocery store and their kids and want something they can't have. Diversions, in such a case, can be considered a preventive measure.

Another benefit of distractions is that it can also prevent children from engaging in dangerous behavior. Ask yourself this, have you never caught them trying to do something that can result in injury? Maybe they tried to get onto the stool by themselves, tried to dig their hands in the cookie jar over the shelf, went near a socket with a fork in their hands, or decided to act like an adult and take the stairs by themselves when they have just started walking. We don't need much imagination to think about how they could have ended up with injuries and trauma. In those cases, where your instinct is to plain-out say "no" or scare them into not trying such things on their own, distractions can be a life-saver.

Strategies to Redirect Negative Behaviors

How do we go about diverting their attention to something else? Is it as simple as relocating them from the place or taking whatever they have their hands and giving them something else? Yes, and no.

As simple as it sounds, you have to be rather strategic with it. If they are on to it and realize what you are up to, all hell will break loose. So what are these strategies that will help you redirect negative or unsafe behaviors? Take a look!

Make Requests Less Threatening

There should be a way of saying things. Your statements about negative behavior shouldn't be harsh or too direct or else children may become defensive. They need to be reminded of the negative behavior subtly. For example, if they are running into the house, don't yell at them to stop running. Instead, tell them that they can hurt themselves if they keep running so fast indoors.

Offer Substitutions

If you notice a fight is about to break out between your child and their friend because they want the same toy, act fast. Offer them an equally interesting substitution and try to convince them of why it is better than the other toy. Remember the example where we talked about a child running with a knife in their hands? When you try to offer them a spoon, you have to convince them that it is better than the knife so that they decide to give it up on their own without you needing to snatch it from them. When situations are handled strategically like this, it prevents misbehavior from happening.

Relocate Them

We have mentioned relocation several times in the chapter as it seems to be a fool-proof strategy for redirection, but it doesn't always guarantee the desired outcomes—unless you are tactical about it. For example, imagine you take your child to the park. Unlike other kids that are taking the stairs to climb the slide, your child is repeatedly trying to come up with the slide and block other children's way. There are two things you can do here. You can either explain to them the right way to go or you can redirect them into going to another swing or area of the playground. The first method, although effective, doesn't always stop the negative behavior. The second, however, does because the child relocates themselves willingly without throwing a tantrum.

Chapter 8: Parenting Skill #6: Treat Every Mistake as a Learning Opportunity

If your child's first thought after they have done something wrong is "Mom's gonna kill me," instead of, "I need to call mom," you aren't parenting right. Children shouldn't have to hide or be in fear of being caught and punished by their parents. They should see parents as mentors and coaches who don't scold them for mistakes, but help them view challenges as lessons.

It has become a norm that we try to keep our children away from all things we think are harmful for them. Although sensible and rather proactive, it sometimes limits their potential and development of skills. When they are repeatedly inhibited from something, they start fearing it. They avoid making mistakes but it also stops them from learning and experiencing different outcomes and emotions.

As parents, we have to prepare them for the unknown. We have to let them make mistakes so that they learn how to avoid making them in the future, and when they inevitably do, they know how to deal with the consequences and regulate their emotions.

The Upside of Letting Children Make Mistakes

It is scary, from a parent's perspective, to allow children to make mistakes. However, if we continue to shield them from the realities of life, they will never learn to stand tall and high in front of challenges. They will always seek shelter behind their parents' backs which isn't the best way to live. Children must be taught to become resilient from an early age. They must be taught to acknowledge their mistakes, accept them and look for ways to get past them. They should know how cruel the world can be, but at the same time, not fear it. They shouldn't panic at the thought of failing, and shouldn't give up without trying. Some of the most important benefits of making mistakes are below.

Children Learn about Resilience

Resilience is the ability to recover from a setback. This is only possible when there is a failure or setback to begin with. As we all know, it is only when we go through some trauma that we are able to know how it feels. Children need to experience the same thing to build resilience. Besides, when they make a mistake, it allows them to look for the reasons why things went sideways. When they think instead of give up, they are also less prone to throw temper tantrums or blame others. Instead, they look for ways to spring back into action.

Becoming resilient also helps them take on new initiatives with confidence. This enables them to experience new things.

Children Learn About Responsibility

When children make mistakes, they are able to see the consequences of their action in reality. This helps them take up the responsibility for their mistakes and encourages them to become more vigilant and smart the next time. For instance, if a child fails in an exam because they didn't study well, they will act more responsibly the next time because the consequences of failing aren't fruitful. Having developed this sense of responsibility is a sign of maturity. If they aren't responsible, it means that they are careless, lazy, and give excuses for when they fail instead of working to prevent them from happening again.

Children Learn About Decision-Making Skills

When we let children make mistakes, it also gets them thinking of the decisions they made that led to the failure. They start thinking about what they could have done differently and what they will do differently the next time. They also learn about how important good decision-making is and what impact it can have on the outcome. As they keep on making mistakes and reviewing the things they did wrong, their decision-making skills improve. This allows them to gain wisdom from their failures and mistakes, and to improve their behavior. This is classic positive disciplining in action because we no longer hold our children back or dictate the steps that lead to guaranteed success. We let them figure it out on their own and take the back seat. When this happens, parents can gradually pull themselves back from the equation and trust their child's ability to manage things without parental supervision. When kids sense that, they feel more independent and self-reliant.

How to Encourage Children to Learn from their Mistakes

Now that we have allowed them to be kids, have fun, taste wins and failures, how do we encourage them to get over their failures and learn from their mistakes? How can we teach them to not lose heart or their will to keep going when they have committed a blunder? How can we teach them to see failures as opportunities to grow?

Below are a few strategies to help them learn from their blunders and build resilience to move past them.

Don't Rescue Them

Every parent's first instinct is to run to their children and prevent them from making a mistake. If the mistakes have already been made, the instinct is to make amends. For instance, if they spilled their juice on the floor, we instantly run towards them to remove them from the place, get a towel and start cleaning it. It is hard to leave them on their own, relying on their undeveloped judgment. When we allow them to deal with the natural consequences, we are preparing them to deal with the fall-outs in future.

Let Them Try

Let them have some time to do things their way. They may take some time to figure out how to tie their shoes or how to use a fork, but let them. Don't try to overtake and do things for them. Encourage them to try once before offering help. This will jump-start the process of learning. Soon they will feel fearless when trying new things and taking on new challenges. Letting them sense independence, and later, victory or failure, makes them feel more confident and self-sufficient.

Be a Good Example

Another smart way to encourage trying new experiences and not fearing making mistakes is to be an example they can relate with. Talk about your mistakes in the past, the consequences you had to face and how you overcame them. Emphasize how they taught you valuable lessons that helped you succeed. They are likely to listen to your stories and take note because they trust you the most. They will comprehend that even you, an adult, can make mistakes and move past them.

Praise Them when They Admit Mistakes

This is one of the most important and hardest things for a child—acknowledging that they had been wrong and blaming themselves. When they come to you and accept that they had been wrong about something, use that moment not to yell at them, but praise them for having the confidence to come clean about it. This will not only prevent secrecy when they grow older but also make them less afraid of making mistakes in the future. When we sympathize with our kids over their mistakes, they feel valued and cared for.

Look For Teachable Moments

There will be times when you catch them making a mistake. For example, you notice they aren't doing the calculations right, or putting their food plate on the edge of the table. Instead of pointing it out harshly in a disrespecting tone, use that moment to teach them the right way to do things. This has to happen in a polite and subtle manner where they don't feel scolded or disciplined.

Chapter 9: Parenting Skill #7: Be Consistent with Expectations

Setting limits can be rather challenging for parents. But what if we told you that there is a way where you wouldn't need to? Would you be interested? The majority of parents would agree that the word "no" has been the most frequently used word with their kids. They have told them "no" repeatedly, and in most cases, it hasn't helped improve behavioral problems. But the reason these behavioral issues arise is that children don't know what is expected of them. For instance, how would they know to respect their elders when you haven't told them to? However, if you had told them about it and made your expectations clear from day one, there would have been less conflict.

Some parents make rules as they go along. It works fine for older kids but young kids need structure. They need to know what is expected of them *before* (Postal, 2011). The purpose is, of course, to limit misbehavior and help parents set healthy boundaries and limits without being nagged at or questioned. Clear expectations set the foundations right. They assist in building a child's patience, resourcefulness, self-discipline, problem-solving skill, and responsibility.

Why Communicating Clear Expectations is a Necessity

If only our children came with a clear instruction manual or user-friendly guide on how to parent them, wouldn't that have made life much easier? The manual would have had a checklist of the duties parents would have to do to raise a well-manned, disciplined, and happy child.

Since there isn't one, we have to find other means to ensure that we raise them to become successful, happy, and resilient.

It all starts with how we want to raise them and what we expect from them in return. Having clear expectations from the beginning helps navigate the road to success. Since they have a short attention span, they often forget instructions or fail to hear them in the first place. This happens more so when we don't set the right expectations. Children misbehave when they don't know how to behave otherwise. A lack of expectations not only undermines their performance but also affects the result. It also hampers with their engagement and focus. Unclear expectations can lead to confusion and pave the way for arguments and conflicts. It can also cause children to get frustrated when scolded for something they weren't taught about before.

How to Set Clear Expectations

We now know that children do well when they know what is expected of them. It offers them the structure they need to do things right. When it comes to setting expectations to promote good behavior, the first and most important step is to give instructions. You also have to keep them short and direct so that there is no room left for the confusion. Furthermore, a lot of times, we give more than one instruction at the same time, overwhelming them.

Picture this: you just came back from outside and you tell your kid the following: Hang your coat on the coat hanger and take off your shoes before coming inside. Then go to your room to change and then brush your teeth before getting into bed. It may seem simple and direct to you, but for a child with limited vocabulary and a short attention span, you have just given them a list of things they need to do in a particular order. Chances are, they might forget a few, or get the order wrong. So, whose fault is it?

Here are other ways to set good expectations.

Make Expectations Realistic

Of course, as parents, we want our children to attempt challenges with confidence and progress forward. However, goals that are far from their reach can become a hurdle. Taking on too big a task may even trigger misbehavior. Your goal should be to encourage them to try new things and take initiatives. The best way to do so is by letting them focus on small, realistic, and achievable milestones. If the expectations are big or lengthy, you can always break them down into several goals. That way, your child will have a few accomplishments to celebrate along the way and feel more empowered and motivated.

Provide Structure

When things follow a set routine and structure, it creates rhythm in the room. Everyone knows what is expected of them and thus, peace becomes a real thing. Putting routines for children allows them to develop good habits when they follow them. For example, if they know what comes next, like play-time after completing homework, then dinner and then bedtime routine, they will be less likely to act out and argue. This prevents negative behaviors from taking over, all thanks to clear expectations.

Review and Reward

Rewards play a key role in the management of child behavior. We are all tempted to give our best when we are excited about the result. It also prevents procrastination and gets things done promptly. But before the rewards comes a review of the progress. The only way kids are going to follow through with the set expectations is if they are being held accountable to them. This requires that we keep a check on them at all times to ensure they are adhering to the rules properly. Reviewing progress can also help parents identify any shortcomings and help their children accordingly. Therefore, when setting expectations, don't leave things to your child entirely, offer support and counseling from time to time to know they are alright and progressing well.

Make Chore Charts

Chore charts are simple and effective. They are the best way to outline the behaviors and actions you want your child to exhibit. Many smart parents use chore charts to pre-plan the activities for the day so that things get done in an orderly and less fussy manner. Your chore chart can include things like cleaning their room, setting their bag, putting out the dress for school, brushing teeth before going to bed, putting dirty clothes in the laundry basket, etc. This also lays out a clear plan for them to follow.

So we now know how crucial a role setting expectations plays in the raising of disciplined and self-reliant kids. We also know that giving them a heads-up will only make things easier for us, so why not start to pre-plan?

Conclusion

The day we become parents, so many things change. For starters, our mindset changes altogether. Before their birth, we were most concerned about their wellbeing and health; and then when they were born, we became more concerned about their needs; and then gradually, when they started crawling and running, we became worried about their safety. When they became teenagers, we became worried about their emotional needs. We have been worried for so many years and all for nothing. Had we chosen the right parenting style from the start, we would have had less burden to carry. If we had chosen to take up positive disciplining, we would have easily avoided conflicts, prevented arguments from escalating, and worried less about their mental and emotional needs. Had we chosen to apply the principles of positive parenting, we would have avoided most of the misbehavior from becoming a habit and stressing us out.

Parenting is hard—true. But we make it harder by doing the wrong things. We don't set healthy boundaries from the beginning which makes them bold enough to demand things rather than ask for them. We don't appreciate or validate their opinions enough which leads to poor self-esteem and poor confidence. We don't focus on developing habits like empathy, resilience, and kindness, which makes them aggressive and unable to regulate their emotions.

Thus, a part of the fault is ours. If they misbehave, we have allowed them to. If they don't listen to us, maybe it is because we aren't telling them the things they would be interested in hearing. If they disobey and act out, maybe we are not focusing on their true needs.

But before you go into guilt-mode, there is still time. Habits like empathy, honesty, resilience, and transparency can be taught at every age. We just need to equip ourselves with the right techniques and resources. As you may have noted, we highlighted various strategies to adopt this modern-day and effective parenting style. We gave you the means to deploy these techniques and prepare your children for the outside world. We laid out the methods to help strengthen the bond and improve family communication.

We hope this brief guide has helped you get started on the right foot and change the way you parent. Discipline doesn't have to mean punishment. You can use the 7 vital parenting skills instead to teach them discipline and model good behavior.

Thank you for giving this book a read. I hope you loved reading it as much as I enjoyed writing it. It would make me the happiest person on earth if you would take a moment to leave an honest review. All you have to do is visit the site where you purchased this book: It's that simple! The review doesn't have to be a full-fledged paragraph; a few words will do. Your few words will help others decide if this is what they should be reading as well. Thank you in advance, and best of luck with your parenting adventures. Every moment is a joyous one with a child.

References

Aria, B. (2008, January 14). How to Say No (Without Saying No). Redbook. https://www.redbookmag.com/life/mom-kids/advice/a2560/how-to-say-no/#:~:text=The%20average%20toddler%20hears%20the

Becker, N. (2019). Positive Discipline☐: 2 in 1: how to handle conflicts, eliminate tantrums, and raise confident children. Natasha Becker.

Benefits of Positive Parenting. (2019, January 21). Royal St. George's College. https://www.rsgc.on.ca/news-detail?pk=998751&fromId=248258

Brehse, T. (2016, August 31). The Importance of Setting Clear Expectations for Your Team. Ignite Spot. http://blog.ignitespot.com/the-importance-of-setting-clear-expectations-for-your-team

Brill, A. (2012, July 9). Creating a Yes Environment. Positive Parenting Connection. https://www.positiveparentingconnection.net/creating-a-yes-environment/

Building Trust through Communication with Teens. (2013, July 24). Secureteen.Com. https://www.secureteen.com/parenting-style/building-trust-through-communication-with-teens/

Caroll, A. (2019, September 5). 4 Powerful Benefits of Letting Your Child Make Mistakes. Simply Family Magazine. https://simplyfamilymagazine.com/4-powerful-benefits-of-letting-your-child-make-mistakes

Couttouw, S. (2017, May 16). Why Children Need Empathy. I Heart Connection. http://iheartconnection.com/children-need-empathy/#:~:text=Empathy%20helps%20a%20child%20regulate

Dallaire, D. H., Pineda, A. Q., Cole, D. A., Ciesla, J. A., Jacquez, F., LaGrange, B., & Bruce, A. E. (2006). Relation of Positive and Negative Parenting to Children's Depressive Symptoms. Journal of Clinical Child & Adolescent Psychology, 35(2), 313–322. https://doi.org/10.1207/s15374424jccp3502_15

Durr, J. (2012, December 29). How to Set Clear Expectations for Kids. Meaningful Mama. https://meaningfulmama.com/day-362-make-expectations-clear.html

Durrant, J., & Ensom, R. (2012). Physical punishment of children: lessons from 20 years of research. Canadian Medical Association Journal, 184(12), 1373–1377. https://doi.org/10.1503/cmaj.101314

Esther Yoder Strahan, Dixon, W. E., & J Burton Banks. (2010). Parenting with reason□: evidence-based approaches to parenting dilemmas. Wiley.

Farnham, K. (2018, December 5). Strategies Used to Redirect Child Behavior. Hello Motherhood. https://www.hellomotherhood.com/strategies-used-to-redirect-child-behavior-5750989.html

Henry, C. S., Sager, D. W., & Plunkett, S. W. (1996). Adolescents' Perceptions of Family System Characteristics, Parent-Adolescent Dyadic Behaviors, Adolescent Qualities, and Adolescent Empathy. Family Relations, 45(3), 283. https://doi.org/10.2307/585500

Learning from Mistakes: The Upside. (n.d.). The Center for Parenting Education. Retrieved June 14, 2020, from https://centerforparentingeducation.org/library-of-articles/self-esteem/learn-from-mistakes/

Learning from Mistakes: Why We Need to Let Children Fail. (2019). Bright Horizons. https://www.brighthorizons.com/family-resources/the-importance-of-mistakes-helping-children-learn-from-failure

Mischel, W., Ebbesen, E. B., & Raskoff Zeiss, A. (1972). Cognitive and attentional mechanisms in delay of gratification. Journal of Personality and Social Psychology, 21(2), 204–218. https://doi.org/10.1037/h0032198

Morin, Amanda. (n.d.). 9 Ways to Show Empathy When Your Child Is Struggling. Understood. Retrieved June 15, 2020, from https://www.understood.org/en/learning-thinking-differences/understanding-childs-challenges/talking-with-your-child/9-ways-to-show-empathy-when-your-child-is-struggling

Morin, A. (2019, August 15). 10 Fun Ways to Help Your Child Gain Better Impulse Control. Verywell Family. https://www.verywellfamily.com/ways-to-teach-children-impulse-control-1095035

Morin, Amy. (2019a, June 28). How Can Parents Prevent Behavior Problems in Their Children? Verywell Family. https://www.verywellfamily.com/ways-prevent-behavior-problems-before-start-1094761

Morin, Amy. (2019b, September 12). 10 Surprising Reasons Why Kids Misbehave (And How to Respond). Verywell Family. https://www.verywellfamily.com/surprising-reasons-why-kids-misbehave-1094946

Nelson, J. (2018, November 21). About Positive Discipline. Positive Discipline. https://www.positivediscipline.com/about-positive-discipline

Ohene, S.-A., Ireland, M., McNeely, C., & Borowsky, I. W. (2006). Parental Expectations, Physical Punishment, and Violence Among Adolescents Who Score Positive on a Psychosocial Screening Test in Primary Care. PEDIATRICS, 117(2), 441–447. https://doi.org/10.1542/peds.2005-0421

Postal, K. (2011, November 11). How Structure Improves Your Child's Brain. Psychology Today. https://www.psychologytoday.com/us/blog/think-better/201111/how-structure-improves-your-childs-brain

Rasicot, J. (2019, March 19). Why Do Teen Girls Dress the Way They Do? Bethesda Magazine. https://bethesdamagazine.com/bethesda-magazine/november-december-2008/why-do-teen-girls-dress-the-way-they-do-2/

Shealer, K. (2016, December 2). 4 tips for cultivating a "yes environment." APtly Said. https://attachmentparenting.org/blog/2016/12/02/4-tips-for-cultivating-a-yes-environment/

Smith, A. B. (2006). The State of Research on the Effects of Physical Punishment. Social Policy Journal of New Zealand, 27.

Stasney, S. (2019, May 31). 10 Smart Ways to Give Your Child Choices and The Benefits. This-n-That Parenting. https://www.thisnthatparenting.com/10-smart-ways-to-give-your-child-choices-and-the-benefits/

Ticktin, D. A. (2018, November 7). Foster creativity. Motherly. https://www.mother.ly/child/benefits-of-giving-child-choices/foster-creativity

Weingarten, K. (2014, December 8). 8 Positive Discipline Techniques Every Parent Should Know. A Fine Parent. https://afineparent.com/be-positive/positive-discipline-techniques.html

Weintraub, S. (1998). The hidden intelligence□: innovation through intuition. Butterworth-Heinemann.

Why Do Children Misbehave? (Better Kid Care).
(n.d.). Better Kid Care (Penn State
Extension). Retrieved June 15, 2020, from
https://extension.psu.edu/programs/betterki
dcare/parents-families/families-count/why-
do-children-misbehave

Made in the USA
Monee, IL
13 October 2023

44519639R00044